W9-AXT-029

So cute!

NATIONAL
GEOGRAPHIC
KiDS

Cutest
ANiMALS
ON THE PLANET

NATIONAL GEOGRAPHIC
WASHINGTON, D.C.

Giant pandas stay active all year long, unlike most bears.

GIANT PANDA

Newborn giant pandas are pink and only about six inches (15 cm) long.

This panda cub isn't very old, but it's already a pretty awesome climber. Panda paws have special pads that work sort of like human thumbs—they come in handy, helping the pandas keep a tight grip on tree branches as they climb. The pads also help them hold on to their favorite food, bamboo. Bamboo is tough stuff, so pandas make good use of big jaw muscles to chew this treelike plant. These jaw muscles also help shape their lovable round faces!

VALAIS BLACKNOSE SHEEP

Curly white coats and black furry faces make these creatures simply ador*abaa*le! This breed of sheep originated in the Swiss Alps, so these animals contentedly graze on grass high in the mountains. Both male and female Valais blacknose sheep have a pair of short, twisted horns and grow thick, coarse wool that people love to pet. And if that's not enough, these sheep have a friendly personality that perfectly complements their cuteness!

KOALA

Looks like this Australian sweetheart hitched a ride on Mom's back. Don't let those cuddly teddy-bear-like appearances fool you—koalas aren't bears. Koalas are marsupials, animals that have pouches like kangaroos. Koalas are some of Earth's fussiest eaters, spending up to four hours a day looking for and crunching on only the most perfect eucalyptus leaves. Their dedication to finding a good meal is still a distant second to their dedication to taking it easy—koalas sleep or rest some 20 hours a day!

SAND CAT

This fluffy-faced feline may look like a domestic kitten, but it's definitely a wild cat! A sand cat's appearance is partially due to adaptations that help it survive in the desert. Its thick, pale coat provides excellent camouflage and keeps it warm at night and cool during the day. Large ears help these hunters hear gerbils and other prey scurrying beneath the desert surface, while large paws and special footpads keep them steady as they slink over shifting desert sands.

WoW!

SWIMMING PIG

Pigs may not fly, but they can swim—and some even have their own island! On Pig Beach on Big Major Cay in the Bahamas, a colony of wild swine roams along the sand and swims in the crystal blue waters. They spend their days splashing and frolicking in the ocean waves. No one knows for sure how they got there, but there's no doubt that these are some seriously playful pigs!

NORTHERN SAW-WHET OWL

Here's a bird that embodies the phrase "small but mighty"! Only seven to eight inches (18 to 20 cm) in height, saw-whet owls use their sharp sight and hearing to hunt under the cover of darkness, swooping down on unsuspecting prey—including birds larger and heavier than the owl itself! The saw-whet owl earned its unusual name because of its repetitive tootling call, which reminded woodcutters of a saw being sharpened on a stone.

RED PANDA

Heads or tails? When you're talking about the red panda, it's definitely tails! This cute critter's bushy tail can be almost 20 inches (50 cm) long—almost the length of its body. If the weather gets frosty, the animal can wrap its tail around its body to keep warm. The pattern of fiery red and tan rings on a red panda's tail also makes it look a bit like one of its closest animal relatives, the raccoon.

GRAY WOLF

Playful puppy or powerful predator? Both, actually! Gray wolves grow up to be excellent hunters, but they're not born that way. As pups, wolves like to play with their littermates. Young wolves have been seen tossing "toys," such as bones and animal skin, back and forth. As adults, they play a more helpful role and alert the pack to prey or danger in the area. Despite what you may have heard, wolves don't howl at the sight of a full moon, but they do howl to communicate with one another, to claim their territory, or, sometimes, simply to mimic the howls of other members of their pack!

Gray wolves can have white, black, gray, cream, or even reddish coats.

A gray wolf's sense of smell is over 100 times more sensitive than a human's.

FLYING FOX

Bats aren't just around to haunt your Halloween. Fox-faced fruit bats love to munch on bananas, mangoes, and other tropical fruits that grow in Asia, Australia, and Africa. Flying foxes do more than eat fruit, though—they help it grow! The pollen needed for plants to grow fruit gets stuck in the bats' fur and is carried from flower to flower as the animals look for food. Flying foxes also help plant new trees, spreading seeds as their guano, or poop, settles in the soil on the forest floor.

CARIBOU

Call them caribou or call them reindeer ... just call them totally amazing! Giant herds of these large members of the deer family live near the North Pole in places like Alaska, U.S.A.; Canada; Greenland; and Russia. They are champion migrators, covering thousands of miles a year. Even baby caribou, called calves, make the journey. Mothers that are separated from their calves will search for hours until they find them. That's no small feat, considering some herds can have tens of thousands of members!

THREE CRAWLING CUTIES

Think creepy-crawlies can't be cute? Think again as you check out these three adorable animals. Which one is your favorite?

GOLDEN TORTOISE BEETLE

Do beetles drive you a bit, well, buggy? Check out the golden tortoise beetle. Also called a goldbug, this insect sometimes looks like a teeny-tiny tortoise because of the markings on its back.

GEOMETER MOTH CATERPILLAR

If insect larvae make you feel a tad squirmy, consider the geometer moth caterpillar. Nicknamed "inchworms," these tiny creatures appear to measure the world as they crawl through it, one bit at a time!

JUMPING SPIDER

Do arachnids make you anxious, sending shivers down your spine? "Who, me?" says this jumping spider. See the innocent look in its eyes—all four of them.

LEOPARD

It's not going out on a limb to say that leopards really like hanging out in trees! The dappled pattern of shade and sun, created when sunlight shines through the leaves, provides camouflage for the spotted animals as they lounge in tree forks or rest along the length of sturdy branches during the day. These powerful big cats climb trees for other reasons, too. Leopards often drag their prey high into trees, seeking out limbs that are strong enough to support the additional weight. This move helps keep other predators from stealing the leopard's well-earned meals—talk about a clever cat!

Leopard spots are called rosettes because they resemble roses.

Leopards make many sounds when they communicate—they roar, growl, cough, and purr.

AARDVARK

If there was a cuteness contest, this baby would win by a nose! Aardvark means "earth pig" in one South African language, but it looks a bit like a mishmash of animals with its donkey-like ears, sharp claws, and kangaroo-like tail. But the aardvark's snout gave the animal its name, its keen sense of smell, and a home for a long, sticky tongue that gobbles up tens of thousands of ants and termites every night.

Sweet!

SILKIE CHICKEN

This dashing bird might look like it's covered in fur, but it's not—it's just the owner of some truly fabulous feathers. A silkie chicken's feathers don't keep their sleek shape like most birds' feathers do. Instead, its feathers fluff out, giving the chicken a fuzzy appearance and a coat that feels like silk or satin to the touch. And it gets better—silkies often enjoy being the center of attention and love to be petted. Win-win!

21

MOUNTAIN GORILLA

This gorilla baby looks as though it may be off to a playdate! Young mountain gorillas spend much of their day having fun: They climb trees, chase each other, and swing from branches. But because of habitat destruction and poaching, they need help from humans to become adults. The mountain gorilla is one of the world's most endangered species. Only about a thousand eastern mountain gorillas are left on the planet, all in a small area of the central African forest.

WOMBAT

Don't mess with this Australian furball! Wombats are tough, muscular animals. Like kangaroos and koalas, wombats carry their young in pouches. But unlike other marsupials, the wombat's pouch opening faces the animal's bottom rather than its head. Wombats spend most of their time digging long burrows with their strong front claws. The "upside-down" pouch helps keep wombat babies from getting covered with dirt as their mother digs.

This bird's scientific name, *Eudyptula,* means "good little diver."

Each penguin has about 10,000 feathers to help it stay warm while swimming.

LITTLE BLUE PENGUIN

When you think of a penguin's colors, you probably think of black and white, but little blue, or "fairy," penguins are penguins of a different color! Their dark blue back feathers help them blend into the water, keeping them safe from predators that fly overhead, while their white bellies against the sky make them almost invisible to ocean predators looking up from below. Found in southern Australia and New Zealand, these birds are the smallest penguins, reaching only about 13 inches (33 cm) in height.

PEACOCK MOTH

Eye see you! A giant peacock moth makes its way up the curve of a small branch. The startling eyespot pattern on its wings helps scare off birds and other predators. This insect's wings are impressive for other reasons, too. Its wingspan can reach up to 7.5 inches (19 cm), making it the largest moth in Europe and one of the most massive in the world!

TUATARA

This tuatara is ready for its close-up! Found only in New Zealand, tuataras look similar to lizards, but they're most closely related to reptiles that lived during the time of dinosaurs, earning them the nickname "living fossil." Their common name comes from a Maori word that means "peaks on back." Both male and female tuataras have these spikes, which help protect them from predators—and make these one-of-a-kind reptiles look ready for the camera.

GET READY TO SAY ...

AWW-DORABLE!

ANGORA RABBIT

BABY TAMANDUA

ELVIS BUG

BABY BOXFISH

SAROTA ACANTUS

WHITE TERN

This white tern chick has good reason to look surprised! After hatching, these tropical birds often find them-selves precariously perched on a tree branch or ledge instead of tucked securely into a nest. Mother terns don't build nests, but instead lay their eggs in a hollow that's big enough to hold the eggs. Once grown, the chicks will be graceful fliers, skimming near the ocean's surface as they look for fish.

Love!

LAMB

Small but mighty, these little lambs are already able to run and jump with the rest of their flock. They also have special bonds with their mother, who will recognize their call, or bleat, should they wander away from the rest of the group. Extremely active and social, lambs are often spotted instinctively playing follow-the-leader while roaming around a farm. Games like this one have a valuable lesson— lambs that stay close to the flock are less likely to get lost or into trouble.

Chinchillas' teeth aren't like your own pearly whites— they're dark orange in color.

CHINCHILLA

Wild chinchillas live in the Andes Mountains in South America. It can get quite chilly on those mountain peaks, but the cold doesn't bother these little rodents. Chinchillas have a remarkably thick, dense coat, averaging about 129,000 hairs per square inch (20,000 hairs/sq cm). Their coat is so thick that it would be nearly impossible to dry if it got wet. So instead of taking a bath, chinchillas keep their fur clean by rolling around in fine dust. Their fur also helps keep them safe. When a predator grabs them, chinchillas can release patches of fur in a move called a fur slip, which gives them time to dart away.

Active at night, chinchillas use their whiskers to find their way in the dark.

EMPEROR PENGUIN

What is this emperor penguin chick squawking about? Perhaps its father's supersmart strategy to stay warm! Antarctica—the continent that's home to these majestic birds—holds the record of being the coldest place on Earth, where temperatures plunge to minus 144°F (-97.8°C). To survive the frozen continent's winter storms, hundreds of male emperor penguins huddle together for warmth, while female penguins go off looking for food. The males rotate every so often so that each penguin gets a turn in the middle of the bird bunch, where it's warmest.

RED-EYED TREE FROG

This frog's gorgeous colors aren't just for show. If a hungry snake approaches a sleeping tree frog, the sudden flash of the tiny amphibian's bright red eyes popping awake might startle the predator for a second or two. Then the frog, which lives in the rainforests of southern Mexico, Central America, and a few places in South America, can hop away to safety, able to show off its pretty—and practical—peepers another day!

So cute! ♥

FUNNY FACES

These animals have some showstopping features that might make you look twice. They are worth a second glance: The unique traits that make them stand out also help them survive!

TIBETAN FOX

This animal's expression might look a bit solemn. But this fox gets the last laugh: Its long, slim snout houses teeth that are long for the fox's size—all the better to catch its prey.

SUN BEAR

Say "aaahhhhh"! A sun bear's tongue can be almost 10 inches (25 cm) long—a lengthy lapping tool for the honey and insects it likes to slurp.

PROBOSCIS MONKEY

The proboscis monkey has a nose for being cute. Its notable nozzle acts as an echo chamber, making its call travel long distances in the jungles of Borneo where it lives.

RED-LIPPED BATFISH

Pucker up! This batfish looks like it's ready to give the camera a kiss. Scientists think that the bright red color around its mouth helps it recognize other batfish.

SAIGA ANTELOPE

This little antelope's oversize snout does double duty! It filters and warms the air that the animal breathes, making it helpful in both the dry dusty summers and the chilly winters of the Asian plains where it lives.

SPECTACLED BEAR

Nice shades! Andean, or spectacled, bears are named for their fur pattern, which sometimes looks like eyeglasses. Like all bears, they are omnivores (they will eat both plants and animals), but they prefer their veggies, crunching on cactus stems, tender roots, and tropical leaves. They love tree bark and fruit, too, and will even patiently sit for days in a tree, waiting next to unripe fruit until it is ready to eat.

GOLDEN HAMSTER

For hamster owners, good things definitely come in small packages! Native to deserts in Syria and Turkey, golden hamsters are some of the world's most popular pets. Domesticated hamsters are mostly nocturnal and will happily spend most of the night running in an exercise wheel. In between bouts of exercise, they dedicate their time to looking for and hoarding food, stuffing bits in their cheeks to enjoy later.

♥ OMG!

KAKAPO

Just look at those faces! Found only in New Zealand, the kakapo is the world's heaviest parrot. Its small wings and large body make it too heavy to fly. Instead, a kakapo "jogs" about the ground as it looks for seeds, fruits, and other plant parts to eat. A kakapo smells as sweet as it looks—it gives off a scent that some people describe as toasted sugar or honey, which may help it find other kakapos in the forest.

LION

These lion cubs are cute, but they aren't animal royalty—yet. They'll start to learn their responsibilities during the two or so years that they tag along with their mother, following the twitch of her tail tuft as it rises high above the grass. Adult females will ultimately do most of the hunting, roving the savanna in search of prey like zebras and warthogs, while males patrol and defend their pride's territory.

Panther chameleons can move their eyes independently of one another.

42

PANTHER CHAMELEON

Not all chameleons blend into the background! With its vivid coloring and helmet-shaped head, this panther chameleon definitely stands out. A chameleon's skin color changes according to its mood—a brightly colored male is telling other animals to back off, while a more dimly colored chameleon might be indicating that it's not looking for a fight. A chameleon can also change its color to adjust its body temperature: An animal that's feeling a chill can turn its skin a darker hue to absorb more of the sun's warming rays. But there are limits to its amazing color-changing ability—a chameleon can't instantly change its color to match any background.

A chameleon can snap its tongue out at about 13 miles an hour (21 km/h).

ZEBRA

What's black and white and cute all over? A young zebra frolicking in a field of flowers in Namibia, Africa. Its stripe pattern is one of a kind—no two zebras' coats are exactly alike. A newborn foal's dark stripes are brown instead of black, but darken as the foal grows up. Stripes don't just help zebras blend into the grasses of their savanna home. They also may help members of the herd recognize each other, and might even discourage flies from biting!

WOW!

ROSY MAPLE MOTH

You have to agree that this insect's colors are pastel perfection! Rosy maple moths can be spotted in broadleaf forests throughout the eastern portions of the United States and Canada. Like other moths, it undergoes metamorphosis, spending its early days as a caterpillar before unfolding into its fuzzy, sherbet-colored glory as an adult. Unlike real sherbet, though, the moth's colors serve as a signal to would-be predators that the moth wouldn't make for a very tasty meal.

45

Too Cute!

OPOSSUM

Hang in there, little opossum! Believe it or not, this animal is going to be an expert climber someday, thanks in part to its tail. An opossum uses its long tail for balance as it scuttles along branches looking for birds' nests to raid for eggs. Opossum tails are prehensile, too—the opossum can use it like an extra limb, wrapping it around tree branches and using it to collect bunches of grass for its nest.

RABBIT

Some bunny knows it's special! Rabbits are very popular pets in the United States. Their wild cousins, like hares, are nimble and fast runners, taking a zigzag path to escape predators. Both wild and domestic rabbits are extremely agile; they do what's called a binky, suddenly jumping and twisting high into the air, even while running!

PALLAS'S CAT

Meet one of the world's fluffiest felines! Manuls, also called Pallas's cats or rock wildcats, get their impressive girth from a truly spectacular coat. This cat's fur has two layers: a thick, coarse undercoat of long hairs, and an overcoat of shorter, softer hairs. These cats can also wrap up tightly in their fluffy tails when they need a little extra warmth. These adaptations come in handy when temperatures drop to minus 40°F (-40°C) in the valleys and rocky plains they call home. If you want to see a Pallas's cat in the wild, you'll need to travel to parts of Central Asia, like Mongolia, Pakistan, China, and Russia. Don't forget your parka!

Their eyes have round pupils— just like human eyes do.

Depending on where they live, Pallas's cats can have very different coat colorings.

CHEETAH

On your mark, get set, grow! This cub has a lot of running practice ahead of it before it will be able to claim the title of "world's fastest land animal." As cheetahs get older, they lose that fuzzy ruff of hair that protects their shoulders, neck, and head. And once they're fully grown, these streamlined predators will be able to reach speeds of up to 70 miles an hour (113 km/h).

AFRICAN PYGMY FALCON

Don't let the size of this bird trick you! Although these falcons are only about eight inches (20 cm) tall, they are powerful predators, hunting for rodents, snakes, and large insects in dry African grasslands. And these clever birds know how to impose: Instead of building nests, they move into spaces already built by another bird. They are good neighbors, though, keeping down the number of reptiles that could prey on the host birds and their eggs.

AMERICAN ALLIGATOR

Smile! This baby alligator needs to grow some more teeth to look like its parents. It won't have trouble chowing down its first meal, though—alligators don't use their teeth to chew. Instead, they swallow their meals whole. As adults, alligators have about 80 teeth in their sparkly grins, and use their impressive chompers to grab and hold prey. If a tooth is either lost or becomes worn down, it is replaced by a new one.

TIGER QUOLL

No stripes here! The tiger quoll's name is a bit at odds with its spotted coat, but it perfectly suits its sharp teeth, fierce personality, and even its call, which is said to sound like a large cat growling, hissing, and spitting. Quolls like to stretch out at home—each adult's territory is about two square miles (5 sq km). They're willing to share latrine, or bathroom, sites in open areas, though, and possibly use their droppings to communicate with each other.

CUTE-OFF!
PETS VERSUS WILD ANIMALS—
WHO'S CUTER?

The pets that share our homes may seem different from their wild cousins. But these pictures show that animals, both wild and domestic, do some pretty similar things. Can you decide who's cuter?

Time to get up ... it's almost time for my next nap!

STRETCHIEST STRETCH: HOUSE CAT OR LION?

Race you to the food dish!

MOST PLAYFUL PUPS: HUSKIES OR DINGOES?

BEST TORTOISE TREAT-EATERS: GREEK TORTOISE OR SEYCHELLES?

HEDGEHOG

This little animal is looking pretty sharp! When threatened by a predator, hedgehogs use their strong stomach muscles to curl into a ball, exposing their prickly spines. They even sleep this way so that they're protected while snoozing. Baby hedgehogs, called hoglets, are born with shorter, softer spikes that firm up and get longer as the animals grow. When they smell something they don't recognize, which could signal danger, hedgehogs lick their spines—the saliva adds an extra layer of protection.

VERVET MONKEY

Although it's born with a pink face and dark hair, this little climber will soon develop the dark face and light hair distinctive to this species of monkey. Vervet monkeys are both cute and crafty. A troop, or group, of vervets uses different calls for different predators. A "Watch out for the eagle!" call signals that it's time to search the skies, while a "Look, there's a snake!" call means to scan the ground for serpents.

L♥ve!

HERMIT CRAB

These popular pets get their name from their habit of hiding in shells they find during their travels. A hermit crab is choosy about new shells, and tests them to make sure their openings are large enough for the crab to pull its body inside quickly. That might prove a bit of a challenge, as some species of hermit crabs can grow to be the size of a coconut!

BURROWING OWL

Whoooo's there? This young burrowing owl looks like it's showing off its perfect posture for the camera. It won't stay like that for long, though. These owls often use their long legs to run after some of their prey instead of taking to the air to hunt. Although burrowing owls do fly, they generally prefer to stick close to the ground around their burrows. Burrowing owls don't usually dig their own burrows. Instead, they often move into ones already built by other animals like prairie dogs.

Shetland ponies, one of the smallest breeds of ponies, average 40 inches (102 cm) in height.

PONY

News flash: A pony is not a baby or a young horse. What's the difference? Ponies are smaller and usually stockier than horses, and have a thicker mane, tail, and coat. They also tend to have shorter legs, a feature that makes them popular mounts for kids. If you're more interested in seeing ponies than riding them, you can visit places like Assateague Island on the East Coast of the United States, or the Carneddau Mountains of Wales in the United Kingdom, where wild pony herds roam. Most of the ponies we call "wild" aren't really so, since they're descended from horses that were once domesticated. But that doesn't make them any less adorable!

A pony's father is called a sire, and its mother is called a dam.

Squee!

SQUIRREL GLIDER

Time for a quick rest! This acrobatic young squirrel glider has a graceful way of avoiding predators. It can glide some 130 feet (40 m) from tree limb to tree limb—even farther if it jumps from a higher tree. Although they use the same gliding motion as flying squirrels, they're not actually squirrels or even related to them. Like so many animals in Australia, squirrel gliders are marsupials, and carry their young in pouches after they're born.

JAMAICAN TODY

Don't move a muscle! These brave and curious little birds are so good at sitting still that you won't notice them until you're close enough to touch them. Even after they flit away, their curious nature means they won't go far, preferring to watch people as much as people watch them. Found only on the Caribbean island of Jamaica, they travel in pairs as they search forest and scrublands for fruit and insects to eat.

RHINO

A rhino's feelings wouldn't be hurt if you called it a name. (Not that you would, of course!) These animals have thick skin—literally! About an inch (2.5 cm) thick—and even thicker in some areas—rhino skin is built to protect the animal from thorns, branches, and biting flies in its African grassland home. A rhino's size is nothing to mess with, either. Rhinos can weigh 140 pounds (63.5 kg) at birth, making them one of the world's biggest babies!

TENT-MAKING BAT

Meet the bat that's a brilliant builder! Unlike most bats, which move into caves, hollow trees, or other ready-made roosts, tent-making bats are agile architects that construct their own shelter, sometimes from a single leaf. The bats chew into the leaf along its center vein, making the leaf fold in half to form an upside-down V shape that looks—and works—like a simple tent. The bats stay in their cozy shelter until the leaf falls off, then it's back to work!

Loons are known for their distinctive cries, which include wails and yodels.

Minnesota is home to the largest common loon population in the United States.

LOON

Climb aboard! When common loon chicks hatch, they're on the go almost immediately—Mom carries her little ones on her back to protect them from predators. Loon chicks are by no means helpless, though. They can dive and swim underwater within a few days of hatching. Once grown, loons can dive down nearly 250 feet (76 m) and hold their breath for up to five minutes as they glide through the water searching for fish and other tasty morsels to eat.

ADORBS! ♥

GUINEA PIG

Guinea pigs are lovable pets ... with a not-so-accurate name! These animals are not related to pigs, and they're not from Guinea; in fact, they're not found anywhere in the wild. But, they do have relatives that live in the Andes Mountains in South America. They also have huge personalities! Guinea pigs will purr like a cat, jump into the air—or popcorn—when they're excited, and whistle—or wheek— when they're happy, like when it's time to eat!

EUROPEAN TREE FROG

This is one *berry* little frog! Only one to two inches (2.5 to 5 cm) long, the European tree frog is so tiny that it can perch perfectly on a berry. Typically found in meadows and on shrubs throughout Europe, these frogs are expert leapers and can spring long distances for their meals of spiders, worms, and fast-flying insects. Some people even think these amphibians are weather forecasters because they send out a chorus of croaks as rain approaches.

ANIMAL SELFIES

These animals look like they have a camera in hoof, hand, or paw as they strike a pose. Which animal's picture is the most frame-worthy? We'll let you decide.

Photobomb!

GIRAFFES

Say "Cheese"!

MONKEY

Still figuring out how this camera works.

CAT

I woke up like this.

SLOTH

GUANACO

Hola, little cutie! This baby guanaco, also called a chulengo, eyes its South American home for predators. These animals "laugh" in the face of danger, alerting the rest of the herd to trouble with a loud, short sound that many people describe as sounding like laughter. If a predator doesn't take the hint, guanacos will defend themselves by spitting at their attacker, then running away at speeds reaching 40 miles an hour (64 km/h).

HARP SEAL

Off the coast of the Gulf of Saint Lawrence in Canada, a harp seal pup soaks up the sun atop an icy float. Born with very little body fat, pups quickly gain a thick coat of blubber. This layer of fat serves as great insulation. Harp seals spend very little time on land, preferring to swim and dive in the cold waters of the North Atlantic and Arctic Oceans.

WHITE-LEGGED DAMSELFLY

What big eyes you have! This animal's massive peepers provide a 360-degree field of vision, allowing it to track and capture prey like mosquitoes and other small insects with an impressive success rate (up to 97 percent). A damselfly hunts during the day and evening, resting overnight with its long, thin body tucked along a blade of grass. Damselfly babies, called nymphs, are also able predators, scouring the bottom of streams and rivers for other insects to eat.

Too Cute!

JERBOA

Nope, it's not a mini kangaroo! The jerboa uses its back legs—which can be four times as long as its front legs—to hop through the deserts of Africa and Asia. Using its tail for balance, a jerboa flees predators by taking a path that zigzags through the sand, sometimes punctuating its escape route with sudden leaps sideways or into the air. Jerboa jumping skills are no joke—they can clear at least six feet (1.8 m) in a single forward bound and can jump at least that high!

BLACK BEAR

Want to hear something un-bear-ably cute? When this little black bear cub was born, it weighed less than one pound (.45 kg) and purred like a cat as it nursed. After they stop nursing, hungry young bears munch on almost anything—insects, nuts and berries, and grass during the summer and fall. Black bears don't hibernate all winter, but they do tend to be much less active, living off the fat they've put on during the warmer months. It takes bears several weeks to get back to their regular routine after dozing all winter. They tend to spend the spring months napping, snacking, and staying close to home.

Black bears' short, sharp claws make them skilled tree-climbers.

Some black bears have fur that's brown, blond, reddish, blue-gray, or white.

BEARDED DRAGON

This reptile is a natural show-off! Bearded dragons, or "beardies" as they are popularly known, are native to Australia. They're named for the rows of scales that cover their throats. The scales stick out and can change color if the animal feels threatened. Bearded dragons sometimes also appear to wave by moving a front limb back and forth. They're not saying hello, though—this movement simply signals to other bearded dragons that they're not looking for a fight.

MEERKAT

Native to parts of Africa, meerkats stand tall, on constant tippy-toe alert for predators such as jackals and falcons. Clever critters, meerkats live in groups and work as a team, sharing tasks like guard duty and babysitting. The groups, called gangs or mobs, are made up of several different families of meerkats and can have up to about 40 members. When they're not hunting or sleeping, they're socializing, grooming, and playing with one another.

79

PTARMIGAN

Forget abominable, this bird's adorable! The ptarmigan (TAR-mih-gan) has a white pile of plumage that not only helps it blend into the snowy tundra, but also traps air that insulates the bird against the cold. Ptarmigans also sport some fancy footwear in the winter, growing feathers that cover their scaly feet. The feathers keep the birds' feet warm and act like snowshoes, helping them keep their footing on top of deep snow.

JAPANESE MACAQUE

This pink-faced macaque (muh-KAK), also called a snow monkey, is found only in Japan. Although these primates do climb trees, they spend more time on the ground. Japanese macaques are good jumpers and swimmers. During the freezing winter, some groups treat themselves to a resort-style dip in natural hot springs. The water helps keep the monkeys warm and relaxes them. Ahh!

81

Domestic dogs
have five toes on
each foot—wild dogs
have only four.

AFRICAN WILD DOG

African wild dogs' large ears help direct sound and give them very sensitive hearing.

Who goes there? Something has caught the attention of these curious African wild dog pups. Each pup's look is truly unique—like human fingerprints, no two pups' coats are exactly alike. These animals, also called painted dogs or Cape hunting dogs, live in groups called packs. The pack's adult dogs work together to take care of the littlest pack members. The adults will also teach the pups hunting skills until they're old enough to join the rest of the pack in scouting for prey. African wild dogs are some of Earth's most successful hunters, in part because the animals use teamwork to find and catch their meals. Cooperation can be so cute!

LEAFY SEA DRAGON

Don't worry, there's nothing scary about this sweet little dragon! These small critters drift and tumble in shallow waters around reefs near Australia. They don't use those fancy fins to help them swim, though. "Leafies" generally go with the flow, occasionally using two barely visible fins to steer them through the water. Their flashier fins look almost identical to seaweed fronds, and help the fish blend almost seamlessly into their habitat.

So Cute! ♥

ELEPHANT

Let's hear some cheers for these babies' ears! Elephant ears do so much more than help elephants hear. The ears' large, flat shape helps elephants release heat on the hot African savanna. To speed up the process, elephants wave their ears back and forth, making them into giant fans. Elephants also use their ears to communicate—the sound of an elephant's ears striking its head can tell other elephants that it's happy!

LADYBUG

Have you ever heard the expression "as cute as a bug"? It definitely applies to this beetle! Also called ladybird beetles, these insects are considered by many people to bring good luck. For people with gardens, these polka-dotted pals offer more than just luck: Ladybugs pitch in to help with the garden, carrying pollen between flowers and eating aphids, pesky insects that do a lot of damage to garden plants.

Guess who? Three masked baby raccoons—or kits—make a totally terrific trio as they poke their heads out of a tree. Raccoons' most famous feature—the black fur around their eyes—probably helps absorb glare from light, helping the nocturnal animals see better as they look for food. Raccoons eat just about anything that they can get their paws on, including fruit, insects, crayfish, and even garbage.

THREE "FAIRY-TAIL" CRITTERS

Fairy tales feature some fantastical animals, but our planet is home to some oh-so-cute critters that look a lot like storybook creatures come to life!

PINK FAIRY ARMADILLO

This little burrower doesn't have wings or grant wishes. It does have large claws, a pink shell, and a fuzzy yellowish white coat—traits that make this animal *fairy* adorable!

NARWHAL

Unicorns may get all of the attention when it comes to having one horn, but they shouldn't! This marine cutie looks marvelously magical thanks to its overgrown, hornlike tooth.

No flames here!

KOMODO DRAGON

If dragons are more your style, meet the Komodo dragon. They don't breathe fire, but they do have toxic spit. Despite that, they're still sweet (in a fierce sort of way!).

HARVEST MOUSE

These mice are so mini, they can both rest on a thin wheat stem. The smallest rodents in Europe, these golden brown mice are no bigger than an adult human thumb. Their petite size isn't their only distinguishing feature. Harvest mice have prehensile tails that they use to grab on to grain stalks as they climb in search of tasty seeds. Their tails also help free up their paws for other tasks, like weaving grasses to form a hollow nest suspended above the ground.

Sweet!

CHIMPANZEE

Chimps, which live in the tropical forests of Africa, are extremely intelligent. They use sticks as tools to "fish" for bugs in logs, crush leaves in their mouths and then use them to soak up drinking water like sponges, and use rocks to crack open nuts. Baby chimps learn how to use tools from their mother. They also socialize with the rest of their troop by doing some of the same things people do, like hugging and even tickling one another!

AMAZON MILK FROG

This itsy-bitsy amphibian may look harmless, but watch out! The Amazon milk frog gets its name from the poisonous, sticky white fluid it secretes when threatened. Native to South America, milk frogs spend most of their lives high in the rainforest canopy. They have pads on each toe that help them grab tightly to branches and leaves. They're so well adapted to life among the leaves that they hardly, if ever, touch the ground!

Someday this young Canada lynx will grow into its oversize paws—sort of. Even adult Canada lynxes' paws are relatively big compared to their body size. Large paws help keep the cats from sinking deep into snow. They're not the only body part adapted to help these animals survive in the snow. Lynxes also have mismatched legs—their hind legs are longer than their front ones. This adaptation helps them jump over snowdrifts and leap toward their favorite prey, snowshoe hares.

The capybara is called a *kapiyva*, or "master of the grasses," in an Amazonian native language.

Capybaras raise their young in groups, with multiple females nursing the same babies.

CAPYBARA

World's cutest rodent? You decide. World's biggest rodent? No contest! Found in the grasslands and forests of South America, capybaras stand about two feet (0.6 m) tall. Capybaras tend to stick close to water—they need it to stay cool and to keep their skin from drying out. It's not surprising, then, that capybaras are good swimmers. They have just enough webbing in their feet to move them along, and can stay underwater for about five minutes. Water also brings these animals together—in the dry season, as many as one hundred animals will hang out at a water source at the same time. Cuteness overload!

BAIKAL SEAL

This seal's story includes more than its roly-poly cuteness! Baikal seals, or nerpa, are one of the smallest pinnipeds, marine mammals with front and rear flippers, measuring only about four feet (1.2 m) in length. They're also found in only one place in the world—Russia's chilly Lake Baikal—making them the only seal that solely lives in freshwater. They spend much of their time hunting for nutritious fish in the lake, feasting when the fish drift up into shallower waters at night.

HUMMINGBIRD MOTH

Nope, it's not a bird! But the hummingbird moth looks and acts a lot like a hummingbird, flitting from flower to flower, spreading its fanlike tail, and even making a similar humming sound. When it finds the perfect flower, it uncurls its proboscis, or extendable mouthpart, to reach—and then sip—the nectar that's hidden deep inside long and narrow flowers.

GET READY TO SAY ...

AWW-DORABLE!

CLOUDED LEOPARD

JEWEL BEETLE

NUMBAT

TELESCOPE GOLDFISH

VISCACHA

STRIPED SKUNK

Awww, how sweet—just not so sweet smelling! A wild skunk's ability to make a stink happens pretty early in its life. Juvenile skunks can spray the foul-smelling liquid when they're just over a week old, about 14 days before their eyes even open. Skunks don't generally spray without warning. They stomp their feet and raise their tail before dropping into a move that looks a little like a handstand. Then, it's get out of the way or get sprayed!

This bird has feathers so bright, you've got to wear sunglasses! It may seem hard to believe, but Gouldian finches aren't dazzlers from the start. Young finches have dull gray-green plumage and grow their bright coats over their first year. Gouldian finches can be spotted flitting between eucalyptus trees as they search the grasslands of Australia for seeds. Destruction of the finches' habitat led to a decline in the number of these birds, but people are working together to help the population recover.

An axolotl can regenerate almost any part of its body.

AXOLOTL

What's this amphibian smiling about? Well, in addition to having that angelic-looking grin, it's also pretty special. Most amphibians go through complete metamorphosis, losing the gills that allow them to breathe underwater and growing legs so they can walk on land as adults. Axolotls (ACK-suh-LAH-tuhls) don't. Instead, they keep their feathery gills and a fin that helps them swim, and almost never leave the depths of the lakes in Mexico where they are born. This means that they're super sensitive to water pollution, and for a while, these animals were on the brink of extinction. Fortunately, if people keep working together to find ways to keep the lakes clean, axolotls could thrive.

Axolotls will eat almost anything they can catch, including insects, crustaceans, and small fish.

GALÁPAGOS SEA LION

Hello, furry friend! Found mostly in (and named for) South America's Galápagos Islands, sea lion pups are born with long hair called lanugo, which helps keep them warm until they develop blubber, or fat. By the time pups are two years old, they will be some of the fastest mammals in the ocean, zipping through the water at bursts of up to 25 miles an hour (40 km/h).

Eeee!

ANCHIETA'S DESERT LIZARD

What a grin! Although it looks like this lizard is smiling wide, it's actually displaying a defensive stance. When threatened, these reptiles try to make themselves look as large as possible to scare off predators like birds and large snakes. These desert dwellers also have another "not what it seems" behavior: When their feet get too hot from burning desert sand, they alternate lifting up their front and back legs, appearing to dance.

MANDARINFISH

Divine to look at, dangerous to touch! The tropical mandarinfish's bright colors send its sea-dwelling neighbors a definite message: "Leave me alone!" It's a fair warning to predators. Mandarinfish, native to lagoons and reefs in the Pacific Ocean, don't have scales for protection like most fish do. They're far from defenseless, though—their bodies are covered with tiny spines. And if that weren't enough to keep other fish away, the spines also make a slimy, smelly substance that's poisonous to predators.

CUSCUS

Who's up for some hide-and-seek? A relative of the opossum, the secretive cuscus spends its life in the trees. A cuscus's tail isn't only long, strong, and flexible—it also has scales on its end that help it get a tight grip on tree branches in its native Australia and New Guinea. Cuscuses even sleep in trees. They doze during the day—some wrap themselves in leaves. This blanket isn't meant to help keep the animal warm, though—it's to help it hide from predators.

CUTE AND HELPFUL

Hey, did you hear the news? Cute can also be kind! More than just adorable to look at, these animals are also there to lend a helping paw, claw, or hoof.

AFRICAN GRAY PARROT

Sometimes when you've had a hard day, all you need is a hug. These parrots are sometimes used as therapy animals because they are happy to be held and petted, and they just make you feel a little better.

AFRICAN GIANT POUCHED RAT

Rats tend to get a lot of bad press. But some rats, like this African giant pouched rat, do amazing things to help people, like sniffing out land mines—and they accept pay in bananas!

SERVICE HORSE

MINIATURE HORSE

Miniature horses are becoming more popular as service animals, a job that was once just for dogs.

Awww!

DWARF FLYING SQUIRREL

How do you say "cute" in Japanese? *Kawaī* means both "tiny" and "cute"—words that aptly describe this rodent that lives on two of Japan's islands. With an elastic membrane between its forelegs and hind legs that stretches out like a cape, this tiny superhero of a squirrel glides silently from tree to tree to seek out seeds, fruits, and leaves, as well as to escape predators like owls.

ORANGUTAN

This baby orangutan may have figured out the best part of life in the trees: just hanging out! Orangutans spend some 90 percent of their time high up in trees on the islands of Borneo and Sumatra. They sleep, eat, and play in nests that are big enough for a 10-year-old kid to stretch out in. A good chunk of that space is taken up by an orangutan's long arms, which from fingertip to fingertip can be longer than the animal's height!

MARGAY

Now that's some fierce focus! This margay—a small cat species native to Central and South America—has probably spotted something good to eat. At home in forests, margays are excellent climbers and jumpers. Their ankles can turn so that their feet face backward, an adaptation that lets the cats walk down a tree's trunk headfirst. They can also dangle by one foot from a tree limb to snag prey from the ground!

HIPPO

Hello, hippo! This hippopotamus emerges from water for a quick breath, but it probably won't stay above the water for long. These giant animals can spend up to five minutes underwater without surfacing for air. They also have ears and nostrils that close to keep out water when they're below the surface. Despite their love for the water, hippos don't eat many aquatic plants. Instead, they come onto land to graze on grasses that cover the banks of rivers and ponds.

113

Rainbow lorikeets help pollinate eucalyptus, African tulip, and cheesewood trees.

RAINBOW LORIKEET

A pair of rainbow lorikeets playfully peck at each other as a third bird looks on. These colorful parrots—found in Australia and Indonesia—are known for their dramatic displays during mating season. They put on a show that includes some pretty sweet acrobatic moves (like swinging upside down from a branch!). Lorikeets are also known for their brushlike tongue. Its end is covered in a tuft of papillae, little bristles that help them lap up nectar and pollen from flowers. These birds are fond of other sweet foods, too, especially papayas and mangoes that have been left behind by other animals.

Both male and female lorikeets raise their young until they can fly.

LEOPARD GECKO

Despite its name, not all leopard geckos are spotted. Some are white, pastel, or even striped. They are about eight inches (20 cm) from head to tail. If a predator grabs the reptile by the tail, it will break off. The tail will continue to twitch and move, distracting the predator so that the gecko can get away. It takes a little more than a month for the gecko to grow a new one.

GOLDEN SNUB-NOSED MONKEY

A golden snub-nosed monkey perches atop a branch high in the mountains of China. In addition to a rather smushed-looking nose, snub-nosed monkeys have a white muzzle and face, with a patch of startling light blue around their eyes. These monkeys are more social than other primates, spending summers in groups of up to 600 animals, and using a complex system of calls to communicate. Some of these calls are made without the monkeys moving their mouths. Anyone for ventriloquism?

ADORBS!
♥

AMERICAN MARTEN

Cold weather? *Snow* problem! Thanks to a coat of thick, shiny fur, the American marten stays active all winter long. The bottoms of a marten's paws are covered with short, bristly hairs. These further strengthen the small mammal's grip as it uses its sharp, curved claws to climb trees and to hang on to branches with ease. Should a marten lose its grip and fall, it can right itself and land on all fours, like a cat.

ARMADILLO LIZARD

The armadillo lizard's sharp scales protect it in a lot of ways, including keeping the animal from drying out in Africa's hot deserts. By curling up its suit of armor into a prickly little ball, the reptile protects its softer belly from potential predators. This tail-in-mouth maneuver also gives the lizard its name, as armadillos similarly roll up for protection.

Polar bears are the largest land carnivore, or meat-eater, on the planet.

POLAR BEAR

Sliding, anyone? This roly-poly polar bear looks like it's ready for some icy fun! Both cubs and adult polar bears are adapted to survive the bitter cold of their Arctic home. Polar bears have a thick layer of fat and superdense fur to help keep them warm. They even have fur on the pads of their paws. This not only keeps the bears' feet from freezing, but also gives them a good grip on the snowy surface. And that famously white fur? It's not really white. Each polar bear hair is actually transparent and has a hollow core. It reflects the light in such a way that the bear appears white.

A polar bear's black skin helps absorb sunlight and keep the bear warm.

Awww!

BENGAL TIGER

This cub doesn't have to earn its stripes—it's born with them! You can see tigers' stripes on their fur. They also have them on their skin! Each animal's pattern of stripes is unique—no two tigers are exactly the same. Vertical stripes help tigers blend almost seamlessly into tall grasses as they rest during the day and as they stalk and sneak up on prey during a nighttime hunt.

CAPUCHIN MONKEY

A baby capuchin flips its view of the world by turning on its head. The playful primates, found in Central and South America, are super social and communicate in a lot of different ways, including by squealing, whistling, and purring. Some of their behaviors are not exactly what people would call socially acceptable, though. Capuchins poke each other in the eyes, suck on each other's tails, and sniff each other's hands to bond.

123

GIRAFFE

This giraffe's not being rude! Even though giraffes are the world's tallest mammals, there's always one bunch of tasty leaves just out of reach. Good thing their tongues are long (about 20 inches [50 cm]) and prehensile, so they can wrap them around small branches and pull off leaves. As for the dark color of their tongues, scientists think it may be built-in protection from the hot sun's harmful UV rays.

GOSLING

Waddle, waddle everywhere! Although goslings, or baby geese, can swim and dive deep underwater just days after birth, they don't grow their flight feathers until three to four months after they hatch. In the meantime, they spend their days sleeping, playing, and eating at their parents' sides. Sometimes groups of goslings from different families spend time together, but at least one adult goose always watches them. Who's up for a playdate?

So cute! ♥

CUTE-OFF!

HATS OFF TO THE BEST ANIMAL HEADGEAR

It's a head-to-head matchup! These pets are sporting some seriously handsome headgear as they pose for a photo. Which one do you think is the cutest?

HEDGEHOG

BUNNIES

Are you ready for a snow day?

FERRET

PARROT

CHIHUAHUA

127

HUMMINGBIRD SQUID

Shine on, little squid! The teeny hummingbird squid is only about an inch (2.5 cm) long. Its bold colors don't match its personality: These squid are very shy and spend much of the day hiding in the sandy bottom of the Indo-Pacific Ocean. At night, though, they shine in a different way. These squid make their own light, using the faint glow to find prey in the dark.

Squee!

AMERICAN BADGER

Peek-a-boo! Found in the plains of North America, American badgers are expert diggers, using their strong limbs and sharp claws to dig tunnels very quickly. Although they eat just about anything, including nuts and seeds, badgers are especially good at chasing small burrowing animals underground. Badgers have a bit of a reputation for being bad-tempered, but they seem to get along well with coyotes and have even been spotted hunting together.

PARROT

Birds of a feather ... ride together? This parrot pair displays impressive talent while rolling on tiny bikes for a fun photo op. Equally impressive are some parrots' imitation skills. Parrots don't talk, but they listen carefully to the words or sounds they hear often, and can repeat them back. In some cases, these sounds include car horns, chain saws, or dog barks!

WHITE-HANDED GIBBON

A white-handed gibbon finds the perfect nook to relax high in the tree canopy. This endangered species, found in Southeast Asia, certainly earns its rest: It spends most of the day swinging in trees and can "fly" up to 40 feet (12 m) through the air before landing. Considered to be one of the fastest primates, these apes can even change direction midair or cross entire rivers by using their excellent acrobatic skills.

CLOWNFISH

It looks like this anemone finds these clownfish pretty familiar! Clownfish rarely stray more than several feet away from their anemone neighbors. Anemone look a little like plants, but they are animals. Their tentacles have stinging barbs that drive away most fish—but not clownfish! The brightly colored fish brush against the anemone's tentacles for hours, or even days, until a layer of slime-like mucus forms along the fish's scales. This mucus protects the clownfish from being stung. In return for the anemone's protection, the clownfish help clean the anemone and chase away predators. It's a cute reciprocal, or win-win, situation!

Clownfish earned their name because some people thought their bright coloring looked like a clown's makeup.

All clownfish are born male, but some become female as they get older.

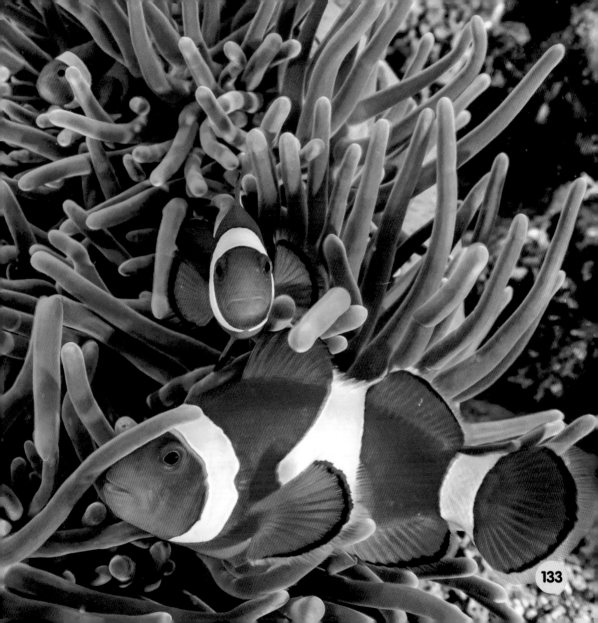

Love!

AMERICAN PIKA

The American pika is one tough cookie! These little mammals are able to survive high in rocky, mountainous habitats, making their home in one of the harshest terrains on Earth. Pikas forage for the sparse grasses, wildflowers, and weeds that peek through the rocky ground. To prepare for bitterly cold mountain winters, pikas dry plants they collect over the summer to nibble on in winter, when food is much scarcer.

PANGOLIN

This pinecone-looking critter is the only mammal on Earth that has scales all over its body. Pangolins' scales are made of keratin—the same material as your fingernails—and help protect them from predators. But the scales, used in traditional Asian medicine, make pangolins one of the most poached animals in the world. People around the world are working together to help stop this practice, however, and to allow these gentle animals to live peacefully in the wild.

GRIZZLY BEAR

Sometimes you just have to stop, smell, and maybe even eat the flowers—this grizzly cub might! To prepare for winter, grizzlies eat as much as they can during late summer and fall, using excellent hunting and foraging skills to snack on a variety of foods. They can eat for up to 20 hours a day and never feel full. The result? In some cases, a bear can gain more than three pounds (1.4 kg) in a single day!

ALPACA

These sweet and sure-footed animals originated in the Andes Mountains of South America. Alpacas have been domesticated for a long time—records of these animals living with and helping people date to more than 6,000 years ago. Nowadays, alpacas make pretty lovable pets. Plus, alpaca wool can be shorn and used to make supersoft clothing and blankets. Some alpacas are even used to guard other farm animals like sheep or chickens from predators.

TWO-TOED SLOTH

If you see a sloth, you're probably going to catch it snoozing—or at least think it is! These shaggy tree dwellers sometimes sleep up to 10 hours a day in the wild. And even when a sloth is on the move, its motion is so slow that some predators won't even notice as it moves through the trees. The reason sloths live life in the slow lane? Their diet doesn't provide the animals with a lot of energy. There's an upside to not always being in a hurry, though. Some sloths are so sluggish that tiny green algae grow on their fur, giving them a greenish tinge that helps the animals blend into leaves.

Sloths often get the hydration they need from the plants they eat.

These animals do almost everything upside down—including giving birth to babies!

RING-TAILED LEMUR

It's a cute conspiracy! No, seriously—a group of lemurs is sometimes called a conspiracy. These ring-tailed Madagascan lemurs like to get close and cuddly. In the wild, ring-tailed lemurs live in groups that can be as large as 30 animals. During the day, they travel in packs foraging for food. While on the move, they keep their tails raised high in the air so other lemurs can see them. This helps keep individuals from getting lost as the group moves through the forest.

BEAVER

This itty-bitty beaver kit looks like it's ready for a swim! Beavers are excellent swimmers and can stay underwater for 10 minutes before they need to take a breath. Their back feet are webbed like a duck's, and their large flat tail acts like a boat's rudder to help steer them through water. When they're not swimming, beavers are usually hard at work building or repairing their lodges, homes made out of sticks, branches, and mud.

Awww!

LOVEBIRD

The snuggle skills of these parrots easily earn them the nickname "lovebirds"! These small birds, native to Africa, mate for life, tend to perch in pairs, and even feed each other. And they don't save all their love for their own kind— pet birds also form bonds with people and will snuggle, cuddle, and groom them by gently licking and biting them.

GOAT

People have known for quite a while that baby goats, or kids, are the sweetest animals around! Goats may have been one of the first animals to be tamed by humans. Goats have a reputation for eating anything because they chew on items like paper and clothing to see whether or not they're tasty. They also help humans by eating a lot of tough plants that other animals can't or don't want to eat, like weeds, thorny shrubs, and poison ivy—no kidding!

PLAYTIME!

It's not easy being an animal in the wild—there's food to find, territory to defend, and homes to build. But sometimes animals need to unwind, too, and we've discovered that some do it the same way people do—by playing!

CROCODILES

People aren't the only ones who like piggyback rides—crocodiles do, too!

ALASKAN BROWN BEAR

Playing in the water isn't just a good way to take a break—it also helps to keep animals cool, and may even result in finding a snack!

144

AFRICAN ELEPHANTS

Almost like a human's high five or handshake, elephants' trunk touches are how these social creatures greet a friend or get to know another elephant.

ATLANTIC BOTTLE-NOSE DOLPHINS

Atlantic bottlenose dolphins are fantastic jumpers. Scientists think these animals jump while hunting, to communicate, and maybe even just for fun!

Pucker up! Baby apes like this orangutan play a lot like human babies—including making funny faces!

ORANGUTAN

PUPPY

If you have a cute puppy like this one, you're not alone. Dogs live in about 40 percent of U.S. homes. And to many people, pooches aren't just pets—they're family members. With a little help from their humans, an increasing number of dogs celebrate birthdays, go on vacations, and dress up for Halloween. Dogs have been human companions for thousands of years, but they still do some of the same things that their wild wolf cousins do, like learn their place in the pack, even if their pack is mostly made up of humans!

SEA TURTLE

Time to hit the waves! Sea turtles leave their nesting areas and travel more than 1,615 miles (2,600 km) to their feeding areas. Once they arrive, they feed on lots of aquatic plants and seaweed. Turtles don't have teeth, but the edge of their mouth has tiny ridges that they use to snip off pieces of vegetation. They eat so much of the green stuff that even their body fat is green!

BOBCAT

These little kitties are named for their short, or "bobbed," tail. Bobcats are North America's most common wild cats, with an estimated population of more than one million. They're hard to see in the wild, though. They are not only shy, but their spotted fur also helps them blend in with many habitats, from swamps to deserts to mountains. And those ear tufts are thought to further protect their privacy, helping them hear—and avoid—an animal nearby.

Too cute!

ROE DEER

A big-eyed roe deer fawn hides among leaves on the floor of its forest home. Its dappled coat looks a lot like sunlight shining through leaves. Those spots—all 300 or so of them—camouflage the fawn, helping it hide from predators like red foxes and bears. Fawns are also born with little or no scent, so even animals with a keen sense of smell can't easily find them.

FENNEC FOX

Fennec foxes are the world's smallest foxes—many are smaller than a house cat.

These animals' feet act like snowshoes to keep them from sinking into sand.

What big ears you have! All the better to cool off with. This animal, also called the desert fox, lives in dry regions of North Africa and on the Arabian Peninsula. Its big ears aren't just for show—they act like radiators, moving heat away from its body, while helping the animal listen for prey scuttling beneath the soil. Its light-colored coat benefits this desert dweller, too. Its pale color reflects sun during hot days and helps the fennec fox blend into its sandy home. The fur also has a thick woolly undercoat that keeps the fox warm during the night, when temperatures drop drastically.

SIX-BANDED ARMADILLO

Yellow, there! The six-banded, or yellow, armadillo can be found in the grasslands of South America. This animal is definitely not a fighter. If spotted by a person or potential predator, an armadillo will likely curl into a ball so that only its bony, protective outer plates are visible. What this mammal lacks in fierceness, it makes up for in other areas. Armadillos are good swimmers, despite their shells. They'll sometimes help themselves float by swallowing air.

DIK-DIK

So sweet and nice, you'll say it twice! These tiny African antelopes get their name from the alarm call that female dik-diks make. They warn not only other dik-diks but also any other animals in the area that a predator is near. Most antelopes find safety in numbers by living in herds—but not these animals. Dik-diks and their mates spend most of their time with each other, sleeping through hot days and looking for fruit and tasty plant shoots at night.

Squee!

PRAIRIE DOG

These prairie dogs look like they're excited for a kiss—from another prairie dog, that is. Touching muzzles is just one of many ways that these social animals communicate. Another is the loud screech that warns other prairie dogs in the colony that danger is approaching, and sends its members scrambling for their burrows. Scientists think that the constant stream of noises from the little animals, which sound like chattering, might actually be a fairly complex language.

SPICEBUSH SWALLOWTAIL CATERPILLAR

What're you looking at? This caterpillar's markings make it look like it could win a staring contest. Its large watchful "eyes" seem to mimic a green snake. When the trick works, the caterpillar is able to scare away birds, keeping it alive until it's ready to go through metamorphosis. It will emerge from a chrysalis as a dark brown and black butterfly that uses yet another trick—it looks very similar to a bad-tasting butterfly.

155

GET READY TO SAY ...

AWW-DORABLE!

BETTA FISH

EMPEROR TAMARIN

IRRAWADDY DOLPHIN

GERENUK

FLAPJACK OCTOPUS

157

A honeybee's wings move at about 200 beats every second.

HONEYBEE

Have you heard the buzz? Honeybees are more than just buzzing bits of flying fuzz—they're also really important for the environment. Pollen sticks to the bee's fuzzy body. After hitching a ride on the bee as it looks for sweet nectar to sip, the pollen falls off onto a different flower. The result? More plants, flowers, fruit, and seeds for animals (and people!) to eat. If you want to attract more of these helpful insects to your yard, plant flowers that are blue or yellow, smell sweet, and are open during the day. And the next time you see a bee, don't forget to say thank you!

Honeybees perform a waggle dance to direct other hive members to food sources.

PORCUPINE

Looking sharp, little porcupette! Baby porcupines are born with a coat of soft quills mixed with long, soft hair. The hair will stay soft, but the quills harden a few days after birth. Adult porcupines have about 30,000 needlelike quills. They can't shoot or throw them at predators, but they do grow back any they've lost. That can happen pretty easily—even lightly touching a porcupine can leave some quills stuck in another animal. Quills have barbed ends that make them a (literal) pain to remove!

OMG!

KITTEN

This bitty kitty will grow up to be what many people think is the world's most purr-fect pet. More than 80 million cats live in households in the United States. The relationship between cats and people is a long one, existing for about 9,500 years. Although cats have been domesticated for a long time, we still haven't quite figured them out. They're pretty good at figuring people out, though, and learn quickly how to get what they want out of different members of the household.

TAPIR

This baby tapir "nose" that it's a cutie! Tapirs, which are related to rhinos and horses, use their noses like elephants use their trunks—to grab leaves and stuff them into their mouths. Their sniffer is also sensitive, able to smell other tapirs from a long distance away. This baby tapir will lose its spots and stripes as it grows, but for now, its colorful coat helps it blend into the forest floor.

MOUNTAIN CAVY

Able to run from day one, these little animals are go-getters. Unlike most other mammals, which only drink their mother's milk when they're newborns, mountain cavies also eat solid food like roots, fruit, and seeds right after they're born. Cavies only eat plants, but they're not fussy—they'll eat bark and leaves from plants that few other animals will touch. Spending mealtimes in shrubbery has an added bonus—it hides cavies from the watchful eyes of hawks and other predators.

THREE (SORT OF) CUTE SUPERHEROES

These animals weren't part of a super-secret lab experiment, and they don't have any real superpowers—but some of what they do is pretty spectacular!

BOMBARDIER BEETLE

It's not a stream of fire, but it's pretty close. Bombardier beetles squirt hot liquid when they're startled.

PLATYPUS

Platypuses look like they're smiling—and with good reason. They can tell where other animals are in the water by sensing the electrical energy their bodies give off.

SPINY ORB WEAVER

Spiders spin both sticky and nonsticky silk when making their webs. The sticky silk is strong stuff, able to trap prey much heavier than the spider itself.

Watch out, insects, I like my meals supersized!

SLOW LORIS

Who could resist those beautiful eyes? The slow loris is nocturnal, so its powerful peepers help it find food like fruit, small animals, and insects as it creeps through the trees of Southeast Asia at night. Lorises are very shy and tend to freeze when spotted, sometimes using their front paws to cover their faces, too. Once a loris stops moving, it may be several hours before it decides to get going again!

You can see right through this little octopus! Although it was born only a short time ago, this common octopus hatchling is already completely independent of its parents. In addition to its eight arms, octopuses have three hearts. One heart pushes blood through its body, while the other two pump blood to the gills it uses to breathe. Having three hearts also helps octopuses swim quickly, cruising beneath the ocean at 25 miles an hour (40 km/h).

ADORBS! ♥

RED KANGAROO

G'day! A little joey pops out of its mother's pouch. This baby red kangaroo has already done some serious growing—it was only about the size of a jelly bean when it was born. It still has a ways to go, though. Some male red kangaroos can grow to more than six feet (1.8 m) tall, making them the world's largest marsupial. As king-size kangaroos, they are efficient hoppers, able to clear almost 30 feet (9 m) in one jump.

JAGUARUNDI

Look at the cute ... jaguar-what-now? This wild cat is only slightly larger than an average house cat—and this cat's name is not its only unique characteristic. The jaguarundi has a longer body than most domestic cats, as well as a flattened head and very long tail. Although many people think these animals look like weasels or otters, they're most closely related to mountain lions. Like many of their feline relatives, jaguarundis are good climbers, but unlike most cats, they're good swimmers and don't mind taking to the water.

Kinkajous are playful creatures—they will chase each other through the treetops.

KINKAJOU

This critter's a bit of a mystery! Kinkajous almost never leave the treetops, which makes them a challenge to study. What scientists do know about these rainforest mammals is pretty sweet, though. In addition to snacking on fruit and occasionally eating small animals, kinkajous love to slurp honey from beehives with their long, skinny tongue. Their love of the sticky stuff and their sharp claws have helped kinkajous earn the nickname "honey bears." But they're actually most closely related to raccoons, despite having a long tail like monkeys do. Kinkajous can use their tail to hang upside down from a tree branch, leaving their paws free to grab their next delicious snack!

Kinkajous pair up to groom each other.

OCELOT

Beware kisses from this kitty! Like all cats' tongues, an ocelot's is covered with little spines. These tiny barbs help ocelots get every last bit of a meal, scouring even the smallest morsels of meat from the shells and bones of their prey. If you think it sounds like ocelots aren't fond of wasting food, you're right—if ocelots have leftovers, they carefully cover them and come back the next day to finish them off.

YELLOW-SPOTTED NEWT

Look, it's a cute newt! Yellow-spotted newts live in parts of Turkey, Iran, and Iraq. These little animals almost never leave the bottoms of the fast-moving streams where they prefer to live. They don't use gills to breathe like fish: Newts are able to breathe through their skin. What's the difference between a newt and a salamander? Not much. Newts just tend to spend more of their adult lives in water than salamanders do.

SEA BUNNY

This bunny doesn't hop—it crawls. Despite its "ears" and fluffy-looking coat, the sea bunny is a nudibranch (NEW-dih-brank), a kind of sea slug. Its long "ears" are body parts that work like antennae, sensing signals in the water that lead the slug to food. Scientists think that the fuzzy-looking bristles on its back serve a similar function. Unlike pet rabbits, though, these critters aren't for touching. Like other nudibranchs, sea bunnies are toxic, so they're best left alone.

RED SQUIRREL

Smaller than their gray relatives, red squirrels are also fuzzier, growing a thick bushy tail and fantastic tufts of hair on each ear. Squirrels depend on their big tails for balance as they scurry from branch to branch looking for nuts and seeds in trees. They make a meal of some of their food and bury the rest for later. Sometimes these little rodents forget all about their squirreled-away supply, but that's OK—those nuts and seeds often grow into new trees.

WoW!

SEA OTTER

Aaannnd ... stretch! This sea otter looks like it had a good night's sleep! Otters sleep in the world's largest water bed—the ocean. Snoozing among the waves can look pretty adorable—sea otters often hold paws with one another to keep from getting separated as they doze. While sea otters occasionally head to land to rest or groom themselves, they spend most of their days (and nights) in the ocean. Sea otters are well prepared for aquatic life. They have water-repellent fur, webbed back feet, and nostrils and ears that close when they're underwater, all of which come in handy when they dive beneath the cold waves.

Sea otters have armpit "pockets"—flaps of skin used to store food and other objects.

Sea otters have nearly one million hairs per square inch (155,000 hairs/sq cm).

COW

Fully grown cows weigh in at about 1,200 pounds (544 kg). This little calf will need to eat a lot before it gets that big! Cows have one stomach that has four different parts. Each part helps break down the tough plants that cows eat. Even with this special stomach, cows have to chew cud—food that they regurgitate and sometimes chew for about eight hours more before it's swallowed again and digested.

COLLARED ANTEATER

Named for the band of dark fur that makes a circle around their bodies, these anteaters are especially shy—unless you're an ant or termite. Scientists sometimes find collared anteaters by listening for the patter of dirt falling from above as the animals use their claws to rip into an insect nest tucked away in a tree's branches. Once a nest is open, the anteater wriggles its tongue into the nest. Then ... slurp! It's time to eat!

BACTRIAN CAMEL

This animal is posing for the camel-ra! Bactrian camels have two humps to store fat and water instead of one, like their Arabian camel cousins. They also are furrier for part of the year. Bactrian camels live in Asian grasslands and grow a thick, hairy coat to keep them warm in the winter. Like all camels, they have long eyelashes that help keep dust from getting into their eyes.

BAT-EARED FOX

Hey, did you hear the news about this African animal? Bat-eared foxes have more teeth than other kinds of foxes. The teeth help them trap their favorite prey— wriggly termites. Their oversize ears help them hunt by tuning in to insects' teeny-tiny noises. Stretching to five inches (13 cm) tall, their ears also help bat-eared foxes stay on the alert for predators like cheetahs, hyenas, and pythons.

CUTE-OFF!

SLEEPING SEA ANIMALS

After a hard day of being totally adorable, these animals have earned a little shut-eye. They look so peaceful when they're dozing. Which is your favorite?

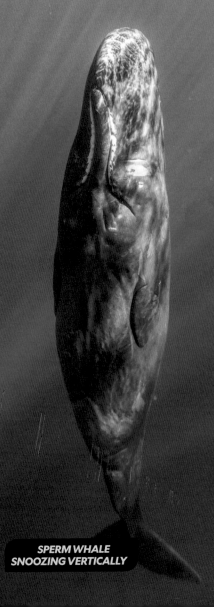

GREEN SEA TURTLE SLEEPING ON SEABED

SPERM WHALE SNOOZING VERTICALLY

SNORING SEAL

OTTER ON ITS BACK

Nite, nite!

WEARY WALRUSES

ARCTIC FOX

Hi there! This adorable arctic fox pops out of its burrow in Alaska, U.S.A. This animal's thick fur changes color with the seasons, going from brown in summer to white in winter. Both coats help the foxes blend in with the ground—useful when on the hunt. If prey becomes too hard to find, as it does in winter, foxes will tag along behind polar bears, eating whatever the bears leave behind.

OMG!

INDOCHINESE RAT SNAKE

Bright-eyed and ready to take on the day, this rat snake glides through leaves as it looks for rats, frogs, and small lizards to eat. The species pictured here lives in several South Asian countries. This snake is at least three feet (1 m) long and is often found in areas where people live. Although this reptile is not venomous, it doesn't really like to be handled, so it's best to just let it go on its merry way!

ATLANTIC PUFFIN

It's not a penguin, or a parrot—it's a puffin! Puffins are seabirds that live along the coasts of the North Atlantic Ocean. They are excellent swimmers and can dive to depths of about 200 feet (61 m) while searching for fish. They're also standout fliers. Able to flap their wings up to 400 times a minute, puffins can fly at speeds of 55 miles an hour (88 km/h)!

COATI

If this little fuzzball's ringed tail makes you think coatis are related to raccoons, you're right! Coatis are active during the day, traveling in large, noisy groups while they look for spiders, lizards, and birds to eat. These groups, called bands, stay together by keeping their tails raised and visible to all members. Members of a band also recognize one another by smell—coatis have glands on their bellies and necks that give each animal their own special scent.

187

A female mountain goat is called a nanny, and a male is called a billy.

Mountain goats are more closely related to cattle and antelopes than to barnyard goats.

MOUNTAIN GOAT

Ready, set, leap! Mountain goats are natural daredevils. They have the skills and body features needed to pick a safe path through high mountain peaks. Strong shoulder muscles help these animals climb steep hills using just their front legs, while a thick, sturdy body allows them to stay balanced on narrow, rocky ledges. Mountain goat hooves are cloven, split into two pieces that act as toes. These toes can spread wide, helping the goats keep their footing. The toes also have rough pads on their bottoms that add an extra bit of grip when the goats are ready to make—and land—a big leap.

Love!

FERRET

Ferrets are some really hardworking helpers—maybe that's why a group of ferrets is called a business? These friendly relatives of weasels and polecats were probably first tamed to help people hunt for rabbits. They've also been used to keep mice and rats away from grain, and because of their long, slender bodies, they've even been trained to get into (and through) places too tight for people to reach.

Can you guess how this little shrew got its name? Hint: Not from its size—an elephant shrew weighs only about two ounces (57 g) and is about 10 inches (25 cm) long. But its snout is quite long for its body. The snout is also flexible, able to move like an elephant's trunk to grab on to the insects it loves to eat. Despite the other half of its name, this little critter isn't a shrew at all. Scientists have found that it's more closely related to—you guessed it—elephants.

FLAMINGO

Think pink, little chick! Flamingos aren't born with their famously bright feathers. As they grow, chicks turn to orange, pink, or even bright red based on the bird's diet. The pigment from the brine shrimps that these birds eat, for example, can turn adult flamingos' feathers their recognizable reddish color. When a flamingo spots something to eat, it plops its head into the water, turns it upside down, and gulps the food right out of the water.

PYGMY SEAHORSE

When it comes to pygmy seahorse parents, the daddies are on duty! Female seahorses deposit eggs into the male's kangaroo-like pouch. When the babies hatch about two weeks later, they gallop out of the pouch in a wild herd of mini seahorses. The smallest species of pygmy seahorse is only half an inch (1.3 cm) tall, but that's not the only reason they're hard to spot in the wild. They're so good at blending into their surroundings that they're almost invisible.

An orca's brain is always alert, even when the animal is asleep!

ORCA

Whoosh! A mother orca and her calf break through the surface of the water. Baby orcas stay at their mother's side for about the first month of their lives—they're even towed along by their mother while they take naps. Mother orcas put a lot of effort into their babies' education. They teach their newborns how to hunt for food, how to communicate with the rest of their pod, or group, and how to find their way around their territory. All of this creates a strong bond—when the baby is grown, it will live in the same pod as its mother.

Although orcas are sometimes called "killer whales," they're actually not whales—they're dolphins.

Awww!

COUGAR

People call these big cats by a record number of names: pumas, cougars, mountain lions, panthers, and—in the case of these little cubs—cutie pies. Cougar cubs are born with spotted coats that help camouflage them from predators like bears, wolves, or even other mountain lions. Young cougars make some pretty non-catlike chirping and squeaking sounds to communicate with their mother. Grown cougars growl, yowl, and even scream, but, unlike other big cats, they don't roar.

Oh, deer! The largest members of the deer family, moose can tip the scales at more than 1,300 pounds (590 kg). Males have antlers that can grow to six feet (2 m) wide. Despite their large size and unwieldy headgear, moose are pretty athletic. They can run at about 35 miles an hour (56 km/h) and have been spotted swimming several miles at a stretch, paddling along the surface and briefly swimming beneath the water.

CIVET

It looks like it's been a hard day—er, night—for these sleepy civet cubs. Civets are predominately nocturnal, spending nights combing the forests and grasslands of their territory for food and sleeping during the hot African afternoons. Far from picky, these animals eat just about anything, including fruit, eggs, small animals, and even roadkill. Although civets have five sharp claws on each paw, they use their teeth to capture and kill prey.

AMERICAN KESTREL

Meet the American kestrel, the smallest falcon in North America. Many of these birds weigh between 2.8 and 5.8 ounces (80 and 165 g), about the same as a handful of coins. They're keen predators, though, and will prey upon insects, birds, and rodents. Kestrels are animal gourmets—once they find a favorite food, they'll choose it over all other kinds. Kestrels usually catch food by plucking it from the ground. Then they'll retreat to a high perch to dine.

TREE KANGAROO

Not all kangaroos are known for their hopping skills! In fact, the tree kangaroo is quite clumsy on the ground. In the trees, though, this marsupial has a different *tail* to tell. Its tremendous tail is longer than its head and body combined. This long tail helps the tree kangaroo keep its balance as it leaps from tree to tree like an aerial acrobat. The tree kangaroo is a good tree climber, too. It uses its strong arms to hug a tree, then digs into the trunk with its back feet and long curved claws, scooting its body along and up to the branches. Tree-mendous!

Tree kangaroos have special pads on their feet that help them grip on to trees.

These animals are definitely the quiet type, and usually don't make any sounds.

MANTA RAY

If you could "fly" underwater like this manta ray, you'd smile, too! A manta's skeleton is made of cartilage, making these beautiful creatures very flexible. They are usually calm and gentle, gliding along as they filter small shrimps and plankton from the water. Unlike stingrays, mantas don't have a sharp tail to protect themselves, but their size often keeps them from becoming prey. They can grow to be 23 feet (7 m) wide.

One, two, three, four … it looks like one of the little piggies got lost! No worries, though—the mama boar can use her keen sense of smell to find her piglets if they wander off. A boar, like a barnyard pig, also uses its snout to root for food, digging into the ground for tasty morsels to eat. Some people also use a pig's sensitive sniffer and super smarts to help find a delicious fungus called a truffle. Pigs can smell these gourmet delicacies even when buried three feet (1 m) underground!

RED-EARED SLIDER

Here now, gone in a flash! Part of the red-eared slider's name comes from its ability to slide quickly into the water when approached. The other part comes from the red stripes found on either side of its head. Turtles don't have outer ears like many animals, but they can hear and often make low rumbling sounds to communicate. Turtles also "talk" to one another by touch, feeling vibrations from other turtles underwater.

Sweet!

RIVER OTTER

Whaat are these river otters searching for? Probably their next game! River otters are some of the most playful mammals on the planet, sliding down muddy banks or snowy slopes, then climbing right back up again for another turn. Underwater, their webbed feet, sleek fur, and long bodies help them roll and dive as they look for fish. Their playfulness is more than just fun and games, though—scientists think that otter play helps otter families practice hunting skills and stay together.

GET READY TO SAY ...

AWW-DORABLE!

TOKAY GECKO

SOUTHERN PUDU

PIGLET SQUID

TARSIER

207

INDEX

Boldface indicates illustrations.

209

INDEX

INDEX

AL=Alamy Stock Photo; GI=Getty Images; IS=iStockphoto; MP=Minden Pictures; SS=Shutterstock

Cover (dog), Pavel Timofeev/Adobe Stock; (panda), Eric Isselée/IS/GI; (pufferfish), Design Pics Inc/National Geographic Image Collection; (piglet), Klein-Hubert/Kimball Stock; back cover (frog), Sascha Burkard/SS; (leopard), Eric Isselee/SS; 1, Erlend Haarberg/Naturepl; 2, Nataliia Melnychuk/SS; 3, thwats/IS/GI; 4-5, Hupeng/Dreamstime; 6, John Eveson/AL; 7, Suzi Eszterhas/MP; 8, Tambako/Moment Open/GI; 9, BlueOrange Studio/SS; 10, Howard Noel/SS; 11, Hung_Chung_Chih/IS/GI; 12, Klein-Hubert/Kimball Stock; 14, Bidouze Stèphane/Dreamstime; 15, Design Pics Inc/AL; 16 (UP), Mark Moffett/MP; 16 (LO), Piotr Naskrecki/MP; 17, Tomatito26 I Drea/Dreamstime; 18, Ferrero-Labat/ARDEA; 20, Martin Harvey/Biosphoto; 21, westcott/IS/GI; 23, Suzi Eszterhas/MP; 25, Posnov/Moment/GI; 24-25, Juergen & Christine Sohns/MP; 26, fotoco/IS/GI; 27, Piotr Naskrecki/MP; 28, Juniors Bildarchiv GmbH/AL; 29, Ian Bottle/AL; 29, Dethan Punalur/Stockbyte/GI; 29, Malcolm Schuyl/AL; 29, Dray van Beeck/SS; 30, Sebastian Kennerknecht/MP; 31, Studio 37/SS; 32, Juniors Bildarchiv GmbH/AL; 34, Jan Vermeer/Foto Natura/MP; 35, Corbis/SuperStock; 36 (LE), Dong Lei/MP; 36 (RT), PA Images/AL; 37 (UP LE), Ryan M. Bolton/SS; 37 (UP RT), Images & Stories/AL; 37 (LO), Wild Wonders of Europe/Shpilenok/Nature Picture Library; 38, Pete Oxford/MP; 39, GK Hart/Vikki Hart/Photodisc/GI; 40, Tui De Roy/MP; 41, Denis-Huot/Nature Picture Library; 42, Cathy Keifer/SS; 44, Tony Heald/Nature Picture Library; 45, IS/GI; 46, Jason Ondreicka/IS; 47, Grigorita Ko/SS; 48-49, Staffan Widstrand/Wild Wonders of China/MP; 50, Anthony Ponzo/500px/GI; 51, Visuals Unlimited/GI; 52, Willie Davis/SS; 53, Craig Dingle/SS; 54 (LE), Olly Plu/SS; 54 (RT), Sicha69/IS/GI; 55 (UP RT), Anurak Pong/SS; 55 (UP LE), Nicole Patience/SS; 55 (LO LE), Stefan Rotter/SS; 55 (LO RT), Konstantin Kulikov/IS/GI; 56, Carmelka/IS/GI; 57, Thomas Marent/MP; 58, Liumangtiger/Dreamstime; 59, Michael Sick/IS; 60, Rolf Kopfle/Ardea; 62, Sylvain Cordier/Biosphoto/MP; 63, All Canada Photos/AL; 64, Joe & MaryAnn McDonald/Kimball Stock; 65, Damsea/SS; 66-67, The Image Bank/GI; 68, Gary Randall/Kimball Stock; 69, John Crux Photography/Moment Open/GI; 69, Jelger Herder/Buiten-beeld/MP; 70 (UP), Wassana Somsakorn/AL; 70 (LO LE), Niklas Heisters/SS; 70 (LO RT), Andres Ruffo/Moment Open/GI; 72, Yva Momatiuk and John Eastcott/MP; 73, Michio Hoshino/MP; 74, Theo Bosboom/Nature Picture Library; 75, Aleksey Volkov/Biosphoto; 76-77, Holly Kuchera/SS; 78, Shinedawn/SS; 79, Thomas Dressler/Ardea; 80, Shin Okamoto/SS; 81, Diane McAllister/Nature Picture Library; 82-81, Jamie Hopf/IS/GI; 84, Mark Spencer/Auscape/MP; 85, Martin Harvey/The Image Bank RF/GI; 86, irin-k/SS; 87, Gerald A. DeBoer/SS; 88 (UP), Nicholas Smythe/Science Source; 88 (LO), Doc White/MP; 89, Anna Kucherova/SS; 90, Ross Hoddinott/Nature Picture Library; 91, Michael Turco; 92, NajaShots/IS/GI; 93, Kathleen Reeder/Moment RF/GI; 94-93, Kevin Schafer/The Image Bank RF/GI; 96, Westend61/GI; 97, Ivan Marjanovic/IS/GI; 98, jdross75/SS; 99, Digital Images Studio/SS; 99, Auscape/AL; 99, Art Wolfe/Mint Images RF/GI; 99, Faustogf/SS; 100, Bill McMullen/Moment RF/GI; 101, Marie Hickman/The Image Bank/GI; 102-103, Paul Starosta/Stone RF/GI; 104, Tui De Roy/MP; 105, Cyril Ruoso/MP; 106, Andreas H/SS; 107, Konrad Wothe/MP; 108, Eric Nathan/AL; 108, Betty LaRue/AL; 109, Dan Joling/AP/SS; 110, Masatsugu Ohashi/SS; 111, Suzi Eszterhas/MP; 112, Martin Harvey/AfriPics; 113, Tony Heald/MP; 114, Roger Powell/Naturepl; 116, Jim Zuckerman/KimballStock; 117, Cyril Ruoso/MP; 118, Donald M. Jones/MP; 119, Daniel Heuclin/Biosphoto; 120-121, Steven Kazlowski/MP; 122, Robert Winslow/Kimball Stock; 123, Pete Oxford/MP; 124, Alex zheezs/SS; 125, Cultura RM/AL; 126 (UP), pandpstock001/SS; 126 (LO), Grigorita Ko/SS; 127 (UP RT), Photographer/SS; 127 (LO RT), WildStrawberry/SS; 127 (LE), chrisbrignell/SS; 128, Constantinos Petrinos/MP; 129, Volodymyr Burdiak/SS; 130, Dave Stamboulis Travel Photography/Moment/GI; 131, Picture Alliance/Photoshot; 132, Richard Whitcombe/SS; 134, Richard Seeley/SS; 135, George Steinmetz/Corbis Documentary/GI; 136, Klein and Hubert/MP; 137, Farlap/AL; 138-139, Suzi Eszterhas/MP; 140, Michel & Christine Denis-Huot/B/Biosphoto; 141, Holly Kuchera/SS; 142, irakite/IS/GI; 143, Schubbel/SS; 144 (UP), Orhan Cam/SS; 144 (LO), EEI_Tony/GI/IS; 145 (LE), muratart/SS; 145 (UP LE), cinoby/IS; 145 (LO RT), Eric Gevaert/SS; 146, Rita Kochmarjova/SS; 147, James D. Watt/Blue Planet Archive; 148, Klein-Hubert/KimballStock; 149, Kaphoto/E+/GI; 150-151, Anolis01/IS/GI; 152, Ondrej Prosicky/SS; 153, Dave Watts/Nature Picture Library; 154, IS; 155, Jason Ondreicka/AL; 156, Pisotckii/Dreamstime; 157 (UP LE), Eric Gevaert/IS/GI; 157 (UP RT), Roland Seitre/MP; 157 (LO LE), Ole Ekelund/SS; 157 (LO RT), Dante Fenolio/Science Source; 158-159, sumikophoto/SS; 160, Tom J. Ulrich/Visuals Unlimited/GI; 161, Antonio Gravante/SS; 162, Tom Brakefield/Stockbyte/GI; 163, Agustin Esmoris/MP; 164 (UP), Satoshi Kuribayashi/Nature Production/MP; 164 (LO), Hotshotsworldwide/Dreamstime; 165, Bill Frische/SS; 166, Reynold Sumayku/AL; 167, Nobuhiko Akiyama/Nature Production/MP; 168, imageBROKER/AL; 169, Arco Images GmbH/AL; 170-171, Neil Bowman/FLPA/MP; 172, Pete Oxford/MP; 173, Vitalalp/IS/GI; 174, unterwegs/SS; 175, Duncan Usher/MP; 176, Tom & Pat Leeson/KimballStock; 178, Nate Allred/SS; 179, Tony Heald/Nature Picture Library; 180, Oskanov/IS/GI; 181, Suzi Eszterhas/MP; 182 (LE), Goran afarek/500px/GI; 182 (RT), Wildestanimal 2015/Moment Open/GI; 183 (UP RT), Moelyn Photos/Moment RF/GI; 183 (UP LE), Marcos Amend/SS; 183 (LO), Ana Flasker/SS; 184, Yva Momatiuk and John Eastcott/MP; 185, Christopher PB/SS; 186, Sir Francis Canker Photography/Moment RF/GI; 187, Claus Meyer/MP; 188, James Hager/Robert Harding World Imagery; 190, Shattil & Rozinski/MP; 191, Mark MacEwen/MP; 192, Solvin Zankl/MP; 193, Alex Mustard/Nature Picture Library; 194-195, Sèbastien Ferraz/Biospho/MP; 196, Klein and Hubert/MP; 197, Michael Quinton/MP; 198, Jonathan Mbu/AL; 199, Tony Moran/SS; 200, Brad Leue/AL; 202, StudioSmart/SS; 203, Simon Gatzka/SS; 204, Joe McDonald/Visuals Unlimited, Inc/GI; 205, ArtushIS/GI; 206, chonticha stocker/SS; 207 (UP LE), Wenn Rights Ltd/AL; 207 (UP RT), Gary Florin/REX/SS; 207 (LO), Bambara/SS

To Elizabeth and Abigail ...
come squee with me. —J.S.

Copyright © 2021 National Geographic Partners, LLC

All rights reserved. Reproduction of the whole or any part of the contents without written permission from the publisher is prohibited.

NATIONAL GEOGRAPHIC and Yellow Border Design are trademarks of the National Geographic Society, used under license.

Since 1888, the National Geographic Society has funded more than 12,000 research, exploration, and preservation projects around the world. The Society receives funds from National Geographic Partners, LLC, funded in part by your purchase. A portion of the proceeds from this book supports this vital work. To learn more, visit natgeo.com/info.

For more information, visit nationalgeographic.com, call 1-877-873-6846, or write to the following address:
National Geographic Partners
1145 17th Street N.W.
Washington, DC 20036-4688 U.S.A.

More for kids from National Geographic:
natgeokids.com

2285924

National Geographic Kids magazine inspires children to explore their world with fun yet educational articles on animals, science, nature, and more. Using fresh storytelling and amazing photography, *Nat Geo Kids* shows kids ages 6 to 14 the fascinating truth about the world—and why they should care.
kids.nationalgeographic.com/subscribe

For rights or permissions inquiries, please contact National Geographic Books Subsidiary Rights:
bookrights@natgeo.com

Designed by Amanda Larsen; Ashita Sawhney

Trade paperback ISBN: 978-1-4263-3921-9
Reinforced library binding ISBN: 978-1-4263-3922-6

The publisher would like to thank Jennifer Szymanski, writer; Avery Naughton, project editor; Grace Hill Smith, project manager; Michelle Harris, fact-checker; Lori Epstein, photo director; Hillary Leo, photo editor; Molly Reid, production editor; and Anne LeongSon and Gus Tello, design production assistants.

Printed in Hong Kong
20/PPHK/1

AWWW,
so much
CUTENESS!

But wait till you see how WEIRD they are!

(... in a good way, of course!)

NATIONAL GEOGRAPHIC KiDS

weird but true!

ANIMALS

300 outrageous facts about wacky wildlife

A newly discovered species of **frog** glows **blue-green** under **ultraviolet light.**

Footprints of a long-necked **sauropod,** found in Australia, are as long as **two skateboards.**

THE NOISE A **PIG** MAKES IN ENGLISH IS OINK; IT'S BOO-BO IN JAPANESE; AND IT'S CHRUM CHRUM IN POLISH.

NATIONAL GEOGRAPHIC KiDS

AVAILABLE WHEREVER BOOKS ARE SOLD
Discover more at natgeokids.com

© 2021 National Geographic Partners, LLC